KU-513-042

BIRDS ~OF~ PREY

Malcolm Penny

Wayland

Dangerous Waters

MONSTERS OF THE DEEP
PIRATES AND TREASURE
VOYAGES OF EXPLORATION
THE WHALERS

Fearsome Creatures

BIRDS OF PREY
LAND PREDATORS
NIGHT CREATURES
WHEN DINOSAURS RULED THE
EARTH

Frontiers

JOURNEYS INTO THE UNKNOWN
MAPS AND GLOBES
THE WILD, WILD WEST
THE WORLD'S WILD PLACES

The Earth's Secrets

FOSSILS AND BONES
THE HIDDEN PAST
THE SEARCH FOR RICHES
VOLCANO, EARTHQUAKE AND
FLOOD

Produced for Wayland (Publishers) Limited by
Roger Coote Publishing
Gissing's Farm, Fressingfield, Eye
Suffolk IP21 5SH, England

Series designer: Jane Hannath
Book designer: David Armitage

First published in 1995 by
Wayland (Publishers) Limited, 61 Western Road
Hove, East Sussex BN3 1JD, England

© Copyright 1995 Wayland (Publishers) Limited

British Library Cataloguing in Publication Data

Penny, Malcolm
    Birds of Prey. - (Quest Series)
    I. Title II. Series
    598.91

    ISBN 0 7502 1385 X

Printed and bound in Italy by
G. Canale & C.S.p.A., Turin

Picture acknowledgements
Ardea London Ltd 25b/Kenneth W. Fink; Bruce Coleman Ltd
5b/Peter Davey, 10t/Gunter Ziesler, 10b/Brian J. Coates, 13/Jeff
Foott Productions, 25t/Gunter Ziesler, 30r/Dennis Green,
30b/Hermann Brehm, 33/Leonard Lee Rue, 39/Geoff Dore,
40b/Nicholas de Vore, 42/Peter F.R. Jackson, 44/Erik Bjurstrom;
Frank Lane Picture Agency *front cover, top left*/Fritz Pölking,
front cover, bottom left/Mark Newman, 4/Silvestris, 15t/Leonard
Lee Rue, 20b/Fritz Pölking, 21t/Fritz Pölking, 24/E. & D.
Hosking, 29b/Fritz Pölking, 32t/Leo Batten, 45l/E. & D. Hosking;
NHPA 7/Stephen Dalton, 8/Alan Williams, 10l/Stephen
Krasemann, 14r + 14-15 + 15r/Nigel Dennis, 22/David
Tomlinson, 29t/Nigel Dennis, 32b/Hellio & Van Ingen, 37/Hellio
& Van Ingen, 38/ANT/Alan Gibb, 41/Hellio & Van Ingen; Mary
Evans Picture Library 12b; Oxford Scientific Films *front cover,
right*/John Netherton, 6b/Roger Brown, 16t/Pat Caulfield/
Animals Animals, 19t/John Chellman/Animals Animals, 21b/Tom
Ulrich, 23/Stan Osolinski, 26t/Konrad Wothe, 26b/Dr Mark A.
Chappell/Animals Animals, 28/Eyal Bartov, 43/Wendy Shattil &
Bob Rozinski, 45r/David Fox; Planet Earth Pictures 11/David
Rowley, 14l/David Rowley, 18/Sean Avery, 27/K. & K. Ammann,
34b/Jonathan Scott, 36r/John Bracegirdle; Survival Anglia 17l/M.
Kavanagh; Zefa 1, 5t/T. Dawson/Allstock, 6t/Kuhn,
9b/Armstrong, 16b/E. & P. Bauer, 17r/Reser, 31, 35/Lenz,
36b/Kuhn. The artwork is by David McAllister 9; Peter Bull 12t,
19b, 20t, 23l, 34t; and William Donohoe 40t.

LINCOLNSHIRE
COUNTY COUNCIL

JN 02599626

CONTENTS

WHAT IS A BIRD OF PREY?

Preparing a meal. Peregrine falcons have regular plucking posts, where they take their prey to eat.

A flight of small ducks darts low across a water meadow, on their way from the roosting site to their feeding grounds. Suddenly, the last duck in the flight disappears, leaving only a few feathers twirling to the ground. A second later, the duck clasped in its powerful feet, a peregrine falcon lands on a fallen tree and begins to feed, tearing at the duck with a sharp, hooked beak. It dived from perhaps a hundred metres to make its kill. Its speed, in the moment before it hit the duck, may have been over 250 km/h. Wheeling in flight, it dived to where the duck lay on the ground, before carrying it to the feeding post. A peregrine is a bird of prey.

Death in Africa

Around the ragged remains of a wildebeeste carcass, eaten and then abandoned by a pride of lions, a squabbling party of vultures flaps and hops. Each fights the others off as it plunges its bald head and neck into the flesh, ripping and gulping.

4

An American bald eagle does not often kill its own food, but when it does, its powerful talons are formidable weapons.

Soon, there will be nothing left of the wildebeeste but white bones. Vultures, too, are birds of prey. Birds of prey live in every country in all of the world's continents, except Antarctica. Many of them are in danger - from persecution by people, or through the careless use of pesticides on farmland.

Tools of the trade

From great eagles, including some of the largest flying birds in the world, to tiny insect-eating hawks - and including the gawky, quarrelsome vultures - all birds of prey have certain things in common. They have sharp, hooked beaks, and strong curved claws - or talons - on their feet, which can close through the flesh of their victims.

The sharp beaks of vultures make short work of clearing up the remains of dead animals. These are white-backed vultures in Kenya, Africa.

The piercing eye of a northern goshawk. Birds of prey have the best eyesight of all birds.

They have very good eyesight, and can spot prey moving on the ground from far above. Most have no sense of smell, but vultures, which feed on the rotting remains of dead animals, sometimes find their food by its stench. All birds of prey are meat-eaters, and most of them kill their prey, with the exception of scavengers like vultures and the bald eagle.

Ways of flying

Not all birds of prey fly as fast as the long-winged peregrine falcon. Some, like the goshawk, hunt in forests and woodland, weaving nimbly among the trees on broad, rounded wings. Others, such as the merlin, fly close to hedgerows to pounce on small birds as they fly out in panic.

How big, how small?

The biggest bird of prey is the wedge-tailed eagle from Australia, which can reach a wingspan of 2.8 m. It is not the heaviest - in South America, male Andean condors can weigh up to 10 kg, and harpy eagles, also South American, reach more than 7.5 kg. A harpy eagle was once seen to pick up a sloth, and fly away with it. When the sloth was found dead, it was weighed at 5.9 kg.

The smallest bird of prey is the white falconet, which lives in Borneo. It has a wingspan of about 15 cm, weighs 35 g, and feeds mainly on dragonflies.

Wedge-tailed eagles were once thought to kill lambs, but we now know that they actually help farmers, because they take large numbers of rabbits.

Fish eagles and ospreys swoop on fish, using their broad wings to lift their heavy prey out of the water and carry it back to their nests. The bat hawk is so agile and fast that it can catch bats and small birds in flight, eating them while it is still flying. The elegant Everglades kite in America has abandoned its speed and power to feed on nothing but snails. The secretary bird - an African relation of the hawks and eagles - hunts on foot, stamping on snakes and lizards.

A merlin skimming over a hedge. Merlins are quite small - not much larger than thrushes - and are very agile predators.

HOW DO THEY FLY SO FAST?

THE dive, or stoop, of a peregrine falcon when it is attacking its prey is one of the most exciting spectacles in the bird world. When it spots a bird to attack, the peregrine begins its dive by flying at full speed almost vertically towards the ground. When it has reached a speed of about 100 km/h, it folds its wings and tail and seems to fall, like a bomb.

Record holders - true or false?

No one is sure exactly how fast peregrine falcons can fly, but even at full speed they can steer to pursue their prey as it tries to escape.

Peregrine falcons are often said to be the fastest-moving birds, because of their dramatic stoop. There have been claims of average speeds of over 250 km/h, and maximum speeds of nearly 300 km/h. One American pilot followed a stooping peregrine in his aircraft, and measured its speed at 280 km/h. Golden eagles have also been timed at high speeds by reliable scientists. One followed an eagle for 22.5 km, and timed it at 134 km/h; others have reported speeds over 300 km/h.

However, when a British falconer attached a tiny air-speedometer to one of his peregrines, the fastest dive he measured was only 131 km/h, and the highest speed in level flight was 96 km/h. To avoid feeling too disappointed, we might suggest that his was a slow bird: on the other hand, estimates by other people might have been slightly exaggerated, just because the dive looks so dramatic.

Stages in the attack by a peregrine falcon: diving flight, the bomb-like stoop and the sudden braking as it hits its prey.

Even staying on the ground is no defence against a peregrine. This one has caught a pheasant that was unable to run for cover quickly enough.

On slow-motion film we can see that the falcon is not falling but flying. It steers using tiny movements of its wings and tail, to follow its intended victim. Until the moment of impact, when its sharp talons pierce its prey like daggers, it holds this streamlined position. Then, when it has dealt its lethal blow, it extends its wings and tail, swinging round in a tight circle to follow its prey to the ground, where it is probably already dead.

When a bird is attacked by a falcon - assuming that it sees it coming - one way of defending itself is to fly very low, in the hope that the falcon will give up its attack for fear of hitting the ground. Birds like peregrines, which feed almost exclusively on other birds that they catch in flight, have developed their amazing braking system to overcome this defence.

Twisting and turning

To turn quickly among trees, as the woodland hunting hawks do, a bird has to be able to extend its wings quickly, to increase their area. The secret of the agility of hunting hawks lies in this 'spare area'. They are able to fly fast with their wings partly folded, which means they can make sudden turns simply by spreading their feathers.

Unlike the falcons, with their pointed wings, sparrowhawks and goshawks have rounded wings, to make them more manoeuvrable among trees. They catch their prey by being able to dodge and twist, rather than by using outright speed.

A chanting goshawk at full speed in Namibia, Africa. Its wings and tail are partly closed, ready to be opened for a sudden swerve.

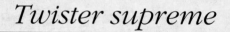

Above Bats swarm from their cave after sunset - a tempting feast for birds agile enough to catch them.

Twister supreme

The ultimate twister and turner is the bat hawk, which lives in Africa and the Far East. It feeds only during the last half-hour of daylight, waiting for bats to emerge from their roosting cave, and then catching them in flight. It spends the night and the whole of the next day asleep, until twilight falls once more. It has large eyes so that it can see well in poor light, and a wide mouth for swallowing its prey whole, head first. Bat hawks hunt over open spaces, such as grassland or pools. This is partly so that they can see their prey better, but also because there is less risk of them bumping into something as they twist and turn in the dim light.

Left A bat hawk in New Guinea dozes and waits for sunset and the chance to feed.

A beautiful example of this kind of bird is the merlin, a tiny, thrush-sized hawk that hunts close to hedges and bushes. It can fly at full speed along one side of a hedge, and then dart over the top to the other side to seize a small bird that it has frightened into flight.

An American bat-catcher

In the United States, the red-tailed hawk hunts in a similar way to the bat hawk, patrolling outside bat caves at dusk. Unlike the bat hawk, it feeds during the day as well, often catching swifts and swallows on the wing. This is not as difficult as it might sound. When they are feeding, swifts fly rather slowly, in order to see the insects that are their prey. When we see swifts darting around the sky in groups at sunset, they are not feeding but getting ready to roost. At that time of day, the red-tailed hawk finds it easier to catch bats.

Researchers catch birds in nets and then release them with numbered rings on their legs. When a ringed bird is caught again, the number on its ring will show where it has been. In this picture, a rather angry red-tailed hawk is being released in the USA.

There are eagles in all continents except Antarctica.

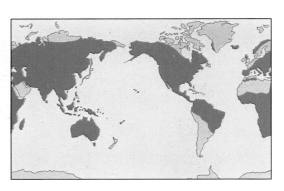

Weight-lifters

Not all birds of prey are designed for rapid flight and swift manoeuvres. Some, like the eagles, have broad wings which can support them while they lift heavy prey. Fish eagles and sea eagles are the experts in this form of weight-lifting. In India, a sea eagle weighing about 3 kg was once seen to lift and carry away a goose that weighed the same as the eagle. Another sea eagle caught a huge carp which was later found to weigh 6 kg - although it did have great difficulty flying with it.

Getting carried away

Many countries have traditional stories about children being snatched away by birds, but most of them are fantasy, like tales of the Sandman, told by parents to persuade their children to go to bed. However, one such story is known to be true.

In Norway, in 1932, a white-tailed sea eagle picked up a four-year-old girl from her father's farmyard, and flew away with her. The bird dropped the girl on a ledge below its nest, from where she was rescued, practically unharmed, by her hysterical parents. She still treasures the torn remains of the jersey she was wearing at the time.

Dramatic illustrations, like this one from a French magazine in 1899, helped to support the legends of eagles stealing babies.

Fish eagles in Africa perform similar feats of strength, though not always on purpose. Because their talons are very curved, they lock together in the body of the fish they catch. The eagle cannot let go while it is in flight - even if it wants to - and if it misjudges the size of its prey, it may find itself dragged underwater and drowned.

A dead salmon weighing 3 kg is easy for a bald eagle to carry away from the breeding river where it died. If the fish had been alive and struggling, the bird might have had more of a problem.

STABBING CLAWS, TEARING BEAKS

Measuring the strong, sharp beak of a red-tailed hawk. The tip is used for tearing flesh, and the sides for cutting it, like a pair of scissors.

HOW do birds of prey catch and kill their prey? Although the answer depends on the bird, almost all of them have certain things in common.

Their principal weapons are their feet, armed with sharp, powerful talons. How they use these weapons on their prey varies, from the stunning dive of the peregrine falcon to some more delicate methods found among the specialists.

It helps to think of the talons as hooks, each foot having one at the back and three at the front. Hold out your hands in front of you, palms down. If the back hook is your thumb, the others are your first three fingers, held slightly curved. When an African fish eagle or an American bald eagle swoops over the water to grab a fish from

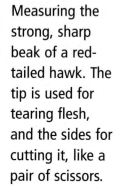

near the surface, its feet are in front of its head at the moment of impact, and the back talon cuts deep into the flesh of the fish. The force of the blow drags the eagle's feet backwards. At the same time, it clenches its feet, so that the front talons also sink deep into the fish. There is no escape from such a deadly grip.

Stained with the blood of its last meal, the talons of a hawk are its only means of catching prey.

Where to eat?

Fishing eagles cannot swim, so they have to carry their prey away from the water and up to a perch to eat it. But many other eagles, such as the golden eagle, feed on the ground, right where they killed their prey. Their hooked beak has razor-sharp edges, so that it can tear flesh away and then cut through it like a pair of scissors. Many birds of prey 'mantle' their food as they eat - that is, they sit over it with half-spread wings, as if they were trying to hide it. No one knows why they do this.

An African fish eagle in action. Approaching its prey, it swings its talons forward (**far left**); immediately after impact they are dragged backwards (**left**); and then the eagle carries away its meal (**above**).

The strangest specialist

The Everglades kite lives in the south-eastern USA, where it glides effortlessly over the swamplands of Florida. With long, slender wings and a sharply hooked beak, it looks like a typical hunting bird, but it feeds only on apple snails, which live in the Everglades. The long, curved beak is specially adapted for winkling the snail out of its shell. The water level in the Everglades is falling, and the snails are becoming very rare. As a result, the Everglades kite is also in great danger of becoming extinct.

An Everglades kite with an apple snail. Its beak and talons have adapted to become long and slender, to help it deal with its specialized prey.

Smaller birds of prey, such as kestrels and sparrowhawks, fly to a feeding post to eat, safely out of the way of any predator that might pounce on them while their attention is otherwise occupied.

A goshawk mantles a young rabbit with its wings as it begins to eat. Perhaps it is trying to hide its prey, or stop it escaping. No one knows.

Eagles are too big to have any such fears. A smaller bird will have a selection of favourite feeding posts, beneath which you will be able to find the remains of its food, perhaps a few bones, a lizard's tail, or a beetle's wing-cases.

A crested serpent eagle in Malaysia alert for movement on the ground below. When it attacks, its long legs help to keep it out of range of its often poisonous prey.

Forest snake-hunters

There is a widespread group of birds of prey that feed regularly on snakes, catching them in the depths of the forest. They are called serpent eagles, and they live in Southeast Asia, from India to Indonesia and the Philippines. Like a smaller version of the harpy, a serpent eagle has rather short, rounded wings which help it to move easily among the trees. It does not swoop on its prey so much as drop on to it. A serpent eagle will sit quietly on a branch for hours, watching the shady forest floor with its large eyes, and then plummet to the ground to grab its next meal.

A prairie falcon in the USA with a mouse it has killed. Small birds of prey usually take their prey to a feeding post to eat it.

17

The serpent eagle has a mysterious relative in Africa, called the Congo serpent eagle, which lives deep in the dark rainforests and is rarely seen. When one was found dead, its stomach contained mostly snakes and lizards, but also the bones of a few small mammals, which serpent eagles rarely eat. This puzzled the scientists who found it, until they realized that the mice must have been in the stomachs of the snakes that the bird had eaten.

Stamping on snakes

There is another regular snake-killer that doesn't really look like a bird of prey at all. The secretary bird hunts on the ground, in Africa. It gets its name from the clump of feathers on each side of its head, which look like a handful of quill pens stuck behind the ear of an old-fashioned clerk.

A secretary bird in Kenya eating a snake it has caught. As the inset map shows, secretary birds live in large parts of Africa south of the Sahara Desert - wherever there is open grassland dotted with clumps of bush.

The mighty harpy

The heaviest and strongest eagle - the harpy of South America - also has the most powerful talons. Its wings are rather short for its size, so that it can manoeuvre among the forest trees, but they are very wide, to give it its phenomenal lifting power. It feeds mainly on sloths - which it snatches from the trees where they hang - on monkeys, and on large, colourful parrots called macaws.

A harpy eagle feeding on a sloth in a South American tropical forest.

It hunts on foot, strutting about on its long legs until it sees a snake moving in the grass. It chases the snake, flapping its wings to distract it. If the snake strikes, the bird fends off the blow with its wing feathers, where the fangs cannot reach flesh. Finally one of its feet catches the snake behind the head, and the bird beats it to death with its wings.

Secretary birds hunt lizards and small mammals as well, and even large insects such as locusts. Although they also take eggs and small birds, they are carefully protected by farmers. Some farmers have tame secretary birds to keep down the number of rats and snakes around their farms.

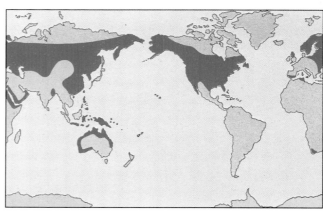

Ospreys everywhere

Ospreys are found on every continent except Antarctica. They live along the shore-line, beside large rivers, around lakes, and on remote islands. The only places where they do not live, apart from Antarctica and the high Arctic, are New Zealand and Hawaii.

In spite of its grace in flight, the osprey's way of hunting is rather clumsy. It circles high in the air over water, sometimes more than 65 m up, until it sees a fish. Instead of swooping like a fish eagle, the osprey drops on to its prey feet first, landing with a mighty splash, often disppearing underwater for a moment. When it surfaces, it carries the fish head first, to reduce wind resistance, to a perch where it feeds.

Jumping in with both feet. Although it looks very awkward, an osprey's hunting technique is very effective

Ospreys breed in Asia, North America, Europe, Africa and Australia, as well as on many small islands. Although they do not breed in South America, they migrate there from North America for the winter.

Ospreys' feet are different from those of other birds of prey: the outer toe on each foot can be turned round alongside the back toe, so that it can grip its prey equally from both sides - with two toes behind and two in front.

As soon as it has a grip on a fish, the osprey turns it longways to make it easier to carry.

Greedy, lazy, and bald

Ospreys are often victimized by bald eagles, which always prefer an easy meal to one they have to hunt for themselves. The bald eagle is huge and majestic - but lazy. In the summer, when dying salmon litter the river banks after they have bred, it feeds to bursting point. It also chases ospreys until they drop their catch in terror, snatching up the meal for itself. Bald eagles will eat fish that has started to rot, and they scavenge dead animals whenever they can find them.

Summer is a time of plenty for bald eagles, along the many salmon rivers of North America.

WHO LOVES A VULTURE?

COULD anyone love a vulture? They look scruffy, dirty and ugly as they sit with their large beaks and bald heads and hunched shoulders, waiting for something to die. Their eating habits - like their food - are disgusting, and they have an evil reputation.

Yet vultures should be honoured and protected wherever they are found, for the valuable job they do. They are the undertakers of the wild, clearing up corpses as animals die. In some eastern religions, vultures clear away human corpses, too, left out for them on top of special buildings called 'Towers of Silence'.

Born to the task

There are two separate groups of vultures, in the Old World and the New. The Old World vultures are related to eagles, but the New World vultures are a very ancient group of birds, related distantly to cormorants.

After the lions have finished feeding, a Ruppell's griffon vulture starts to clear up the remains of a wildebeest.

Right Its bald head and neck smeared with blood, a Nubian vulture in Africa warns off a rival from a carcass.

Inset map Old World vultures live all over Africa and the warmer parts of Europe, and in most of southern Asia, but not in Malaysia or Australasia. New World vultures are found in the Americas, from southern Canada to the tip of South America.

TV dinners

The most common vulture in North America is the turkey vulture, which feeds along main roads and highways, eating the remains of animals that have been killed by cars. Because of this, dead animals on roads in the United States are often called 'TV Dinners', where TV stands not for television but turkey vulture.

Dinner is served: a red-shouldered hawk, killed by a car, is about to become a turkey vulture's next meal.

The two groups have several things in common, however, which suit them to their grisly work. Their bald heads are an adaptation to feeding inside rotting carcasses. Feathers would become clotted with blood, and liable to become infected; skin is easier to keep clean. The beaks of New World vultures are too weak to tear flesh until it has begun to rot, and those of the Old World vultures are not much stronger.

Both groups are expert at soaring - gliding through the air using rising air currents to keep them aloft. They can use this technique as a way of finding food. With their excellent eyesight, they can see when another vulture far away dives on food, and glide over to join in the feast from several kilometres away.

Right Intensive care: a pair of Californian condors in the captive breeding unit at the San Diego Wild Animal Park in the USA. It is hoped that they will produce young that can be released into the wild.

Giant gliders

The world's biggest vultures are the condors. There are two species, one from California in the United States and the other from the Andes mountains of South America. With a wingspan of over 3 m, and weighing up to 5 kg, both species are too big to have natural enemies. Yet they are both in danger of extinction, mostly because of the activities of humans.

An Andean condor soars above the plains of Argentina, South America, surveying the ground for dead cattle

The Californian condor is the most endangered of the two. When miners poured into California in the gold rush of 1849, there were still plenty of condors to be seen in the mountains. But the numbers have been falling ever since, and today there are only about six pairs still breeding in the wild. They are difficult to rear in captivity, but people are trying, so that one day the offspring of the captive birds can be released in a suitable place.

Andean condors gather around the body of a dead cow on a ranch in Ecuador, South America.

Safer in the Andes

The Andean condor is not so endangered as the Californian. Not only are there far fewer people in the places where it lives, but those who are there supply it with food, without knowing it. They are mostly cattle ranchers, and they only round up their herds once a year. This means that all year round cattle are dying from natural causes, without people to look after them. The condors, like all good vultures, clean up the remains.

Why kill condors?

One reason for the decline of the condors was shooting by hunters, not for food or sport, but from curiosity, because they are so big. Another was poisoning. Farmers would put down poisoned bait to kill wolves and coyotes, by injecting a dead cow with strychnine. When a condor came down to scavenge the cow, it would be killed by the poison. Some condors starved to death, because their usual food - dead deer and elk - was hard to find once the country had been taken over by cattle ranchers and their herds. The survivors bred so slowly that they could not replace the birds that had died. Condors breed for the first time when they are six years old, and then lay only one egg each year.

This Californian condor is one of only about 12 surviving in the wild.

Ostrich eggs are too thick for an Egyptian vulture to break with its beak. To overcome this problem, the vultures have learned how to crack the eggs using stones.

Pharaoh's chicken

The Old World vultures look very like those from the New World, though they are not closely related to them. The smallest is the Egyptian vulture, found all over Africa and Arabia and across to India. It has lived near people for a very long time - the ancient Egyptians gave it the nickname 'Pharaoh's Chicken'.

The Egyptian vulture has the knack of breaking open large eggs by throwing stones at them. If it finds an unattended ostrich nest, it will pick up a stone and hit one of the eggs with it until the shell breaks. Other Egyptian vultures then rush over to join in the feast.

The biggest bird ever

The biggest flying bird that ever lived was a condor, which has been given the name Teratornis incredibilis, *which means 'the incredible giant bird'. Its fossil remains have been found in Nevada, USA, in rocks that are about four million years old. Its wingspan was nearly 6 m.*

Who killed the playwright?

The ancient Greek playwright Aeschylus died suddenly when a tortoise fell on his bald head. The naturalist Pliny wrote that it was dropped by an eagle, but this was thought to be a myth until somebody saw a bearded vulture dropping a tortoise from a great height to kill it for food. The bird must have mistaken the writer's head for a rock. Bearded vultures are now rare in Greece, but can still be seen in northern parts of the country and in neighbouring Albania.

The bearded vulture gets its name from the tufts at the base of its bill.

The bone-breaker

The lammergeier lives in southern Europe and Asia. Its name is German for 'lamb vulture', although it isn't a vulture at all, but a kite. And it doesn't eat lambs, although many lammergeiers have been killed because farmers think they do. A better name for it is the 'bearded vulture' (bart-geier), from the tufts of feathers under its bill. Its scientific name *Gypaetus barbatus* means 'vulture-eagle with a beard'. Bearded vultures eat bones, which they collect when all the other vultures have finished eating. They swallow small bones whole, but they smash big bones by carrying them up as high as 60 m into the air and dropping them on to rocks. The vulture then flies down and eats the bone-marrow, and the fragments of bone as well.

A bearded vulture drives a lanner falcon away from its nest, high in the mountains of South Africa. When the vulture's chicks are small, they are vulnerable to predators.

Teamwork

The largest of the African vultures, with a wingspan of 2.5 m, is the lappet-faced vulture. Next in size come the white-backed vulture, and the griffon vulture. Without meaning to, these three species work as a team.

The lappet-faced vulture is the only one of the three that is powerful enough to rip open a fresh-ly-dead carcass. So, its smaller relatives often have to wait for their food until a lappet-faced vulture arrives to 'unwrap' it for them. But if a hyena is first on the scene, it will open up the carcass and the smaller vultures can start feeding. If a lappet-faced vulture arrives after the others have start-ed feeding, it makes sure it doesn't miss out on the meal. Lurking at the edge of the crowd, it waits until a griffon or white-backed vulture comes out with a piece of meat too big to swallow, and steals it.

A lappet-faced vulture feeds on a zebra carcass. In the background griffon vultures wait their turn to eat.

NESTS, EGGS AND CHICKS

Below American bald eagles nest in the same place year after year. This nest, in a pine tree in Florida, USA, may have been in use for 20 years.

S OME birds of prey hardly build a nest at all, but simply gather a few sticks to stop their eggs rolling off the ledge where they lay them. Others take over the nest of another bird when it has finished with it. A few birds of prey build large, conspicuous nests, but they are the minority.

The most spectacular nests are those of the large eagles. Like most birds of prey, bald eagles mate for life. Each pair returns year after year to the same nest, adding a few sticks each time. These huge piles of sticks become landmarks to local people.

Below This peregrine falcon is nesting on a rocky ledge, with only a few twigs to support her eggs.

Ospreys in Europe nest in living trees, and return every year to the same site. The pair display to each other to renew the bond between them before they produce eggs.

When the bald eagle became rare in most of the United States, the nests lingered on long after the birds that had built them were dead - rather like tombstones to remind people of what they had lost. Now that the bald eagle is recovering and returning to its old hunting grounds, some of the deserted nests are growing again, as the birds add new sticks to the ruins.

Long-lived ospreys

Ospreys live for a very long time. They are much smaller than eagles, but their nests are nearly as big. Ospreys gather branches as much as 1.5 m long, wedging them into the fork of a dead tree in the USA, or a living pine tree in Europe.

Sparks flying

Both eagles and ospreys often build their large, untidy nests on electricity pylons. This sometimes leads to disaster for the birds, when part of a nest touches one of the power cables. To prevent this from happening, special platforms are added to the pylons, so that the birds can build their nests out of the way of the cables.

Above Ospreys nesting near power lines in Florida, USA.

Below A female Montague's harrier returning to her nest in a cornfield in France.

The middle of the nest is lined with softer material, often seaweed. Like eagles, the birds return year after year, and often add more material to their nests. Some nests have been used every year for more than 40 years, probably by the same pair of birds.

Ground level nests

Where there are no trees, ospreys have to nest on the ground. Some birds of prey do this all the time. Harriers, or marsh hawks, build a platform of grass and other soft-stemmed plants to keep their eggs dry. Falcons do not build nests at all. Some of them find a hollow among tufts of grass, while others choose a ledge high on a cliff, in the same way as a golden eagle selects its eyrie, where any enemies can be seen coming from a long way off. These birds defend their eggs and chicks very fiercely, attacking anything - or anybody - who comes too near.

Right Golden eagles normally nest on ledges high on cliffs. Tree nests like this one are rare.

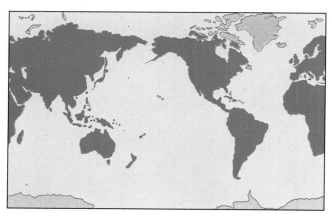

Hawks and falcons are found over most of the world's land surface, excluding Antarctica. Gyrfalcons, the largest of all falcons, breed in the Arctic regions of North America and Europe, but spend the winter further south, travelling as far as Maine in the USA or Portugal in Europe.

Second-hand homes

For birds that do not build their own nests, the nests of other birds are very convenient. Honey buzzards often take over the nests of goshawks when the goshawks have finished breeding. The grey kestrel in Africa almost always breeds in the enormous nest built by a hammer-headed stork, when the storks have moved away. The smallest of all the falcons, known as pygmy falcons or falconets, usually nest in old woodpecker holes. There is plenty of room for them: the smallest falconet is only 15 cm long.

A savage childhood

Bigger birds of prey lay fewer eggs than smaller ones. Eagles and ospreys never lay more than two or three, while harriers and small falcons may lay five or six. How many of the chicks survive to fly from the nest depends on how much food the parents can find.

The disused nests of hammer-headed storks provide homes for a variety of other creatures, including grey kestrels. This nest in Kenya, Africa, is more than a metre across.

When prey is in short supply, the young birds do not share what food there is: they fight for it. The battle becomes more and more one-sided, as the chicks that get the food grow bigger than their hungry brothers and sisters, and win even more food. The smaller chicks eventually starve to death.

Why do the parents bother to produce five eggs, if only two of them will produce flying young? The answer is that in a season when there is plenty of food, more of the young will be able to survive. If the parents had not laid the eggs, they would not have been able to take advantage of the abundance of prey.

A goshawk chick begs for food from its parents. If it has stronger brothers and sisters, it will probably not get enough food to survive.

The biggest nests in the world

A famous bald eagle nest, in the state of Ohio, USA, was used for more than 35 years, possibly by the young of the original builders after their parents had died. It was more than 2.5 m across, and nearly 4 m deep when it was blown to the ground in a storm, and it weighed 1.8 tonnes. In Florida, another even bigger nest was 2.9 m wide, and more than 6 m deep.

Quick little fathers

For birds that hunt relatively slow-moving prey such as sloths or rabbits, it is an advantage to be big and strong. This enables them to kill and carry away the biggest animals they can find, collecting more food for themselves and their families with each catch.

When the prey moves quickly, it is an advantage for the hunter to be more agile, which usually means being smaller. Falcons and sparrowhawks need to be very agile, because they catch flying birds. On the other hand, to produce decent-sized eggs and to defend her young, the bigger a female is, the better. Larger eggs produce larger young with a better chance of survival.

Because of this, the adults of bird-hunting species are different sizes. The male is smaller, so that he can hunt successfully and bring food to his large mate, while she incubates the eggs, and distributes the food he brings to the chicks when they hatch.

Young peregrines have to be fed by their parents even after they leave the nest, until they learn to hunt food for themselves.

A young golden eagle attacks a hare. While it was learning to hunt, it would have chosen much smaller prey.

After hovering patiently high above the ground, a kestrel drops on to a mouse in the grass.

Male falcons are called 'tercels', which means 'thirds', because they are a third smaller than the females. (People used to think that this was because they hatched from the third egg to be laid.) Sparrowhawks have an even greater size difference: the females are twice the size of the males.

One egg too many?

Some species of birds of prey, including the harpy eagle and the golden eagle, seem to lay one more egg than they need. They produce just two eggs, which hatch in the order in which they were laid, a few days apart. As soon as it is strong enough, the older chick always kills its younger brother or sister, no matter how much food there is.

No one is sure why this happens. It may be because it is too risky to lay only one egg, in case it fails to hatch for some reason. It would also be risky to try to feed two chicks until they grow up, in case neither of them gets enough food to survive.

ENEMIES AND FRIENDS

THE only real enemies of birds of prey are humans. Ever since farming began, people have hunted them because they have seen them as rivals, or even enemies. Some farmers still accuse large eagles and vultures of killing lambs and calves, and gamekeepers persecute smaller birds of prey for taking the chicks of game birds such as pheasants. Although they are illegal in most developed countries, many different kinds of traps, snares, and poisons are still being used in the war against birds of prey.

A change of heart

Today most people's attitudes have changed, and birds of prey are respected and admired. However, just as this change of heart was taking place, in the 1960s, a new form of death began to stalk the birds of prey. It had its worst effects in just those developed countries where the birds were at last being protected, because that was where the methods of agriculture were more advanced. Pesticides, designed to kill insects and fungi that were damaging farm crops, found their way into the food chain.

Even though wedge-tailed eagles are known to kill hundreds of rabbits - one of worst pests on Australian farms - some farmers still believe they kill lambs. So, they shoot them and hang them on their fences to deter others.

38

Poisoned bait kills every animal that eats it. In Scotland, a great black-backed gull and a golden eagle have both been killed after eating a poisoned rabbit, which was probably meant to kill foxes.

Timber is a very valuable crop in North America, and growers spend a lot of money spraying trees to protect them from pests such as the budworm moth. Killing the moths also destroys most other insects, and removes important food from the food chain.

The pyramid of death

Although most modern pesticides are less harmful, early chemicals, such as DDT and dieldrin, caused serious casualties. The chemists who invented them and the farmers who used them did not realize how long the poisons would last, or how they would accumulate as they moved up the food chain.

Kestrel

Shrew

Lettuce

Violet ground beetle

Slug

Imagine a lettuce being sprayed with DDT to kill slugs. Each slug that eats part of the leaf takes in a small dose of poison, and eventually becomes ill.

Above This illustration shows how a dose of pesticide intended to protect lettuces from slugs, can also kill kestrels.

A violet ground beetle then eats several of the slugs and takes in several doses of poison. The beetle is eaten by a shrew which, in turn, is eaten by a hungry kestrel. Over the next few days, it catches and eats several more shrews. The kestrel now contains the poison from all the slugs eaten by all the beetles Even if it does not die, the kestrel will certainly be ill, and its eggs will be affected by the poison that was sprayed to protect the lettuces.

Poison rivers

Agricultural pesticides affect birds of prey in another way. When fields are sprayed with pesticide, some of the chemicals are washed off the land and eventually they find their way into lakes and rivers. The pesticide remains poisonous for a very long time before it breaks down, and it accumulates rapidly in all the creatures that live in the water.

Scientists who measured the concentration of DDT in a lake on Long Island, New York, in the USA found that it was quite low, and apparently safe. However, when they measured how much was in the water plants and plankton in the lake, they found that it was 800 times more.

This golden eagle chick did not survive long enough to hatch. When scientists examined it, they found it had been killed by pesticides that were passed on from its mother.

When they caught some of the small fish that eat the water plants, they found that the DDT was 6,000 times stronger in them than in the water. Bigger fish, which had eaten the small fish, contained 33,000 times as much poison as the water, and a bird that ate the big fish could be carrying a dose nearly half a million times stronger.

Vultures return

The bearded vulture, or lammergeier - the spectacular bone-breaker that once lived all across Europe's mountainous areas - is now very rare because it has been persecuted by farmers who thought it stole their lambs. Bird-lovers in France, Switzerland and Austria decided to band together to reintroduce the bearded vulture to the Alps. Breeding the birds in captivity was relatively easy. With the right food, and careful looking after, the birds multiplied to the point where they could be released in suitable places.

Right Some birds are more fortunate than others. This young peregrine falcon is recovering from shotgun wounds in a bird hospital in Colorado, USA. When it is completely well, it will be released.

Bearded vultures breeding in Basel Zoo, Switzerland. When their eggs hatch, the chicks will be released in the wild.

Falconry is a very old tradition in Arab countries. In Saudi Arabia, falconers gather regularly to buy and sell birds.

The next step was to carry the young birds high into the mountains, to put them in the sort of cave where they might have hatched in the wild. They were then given bones and scraps of meat to eat, until they grew their feathers and began to fly.

Today there are a dozen or more bearded vultures flying over Austria, and others in France and Switzerland. The last stage of the operation to save them is to persuade farmers to think of the birds as bearded vultures, and not as 'lamb-vultures'. One has already been found shot, but when the new name is accepted it could make the difference between life and death for the bearded vulture.

Colourful killers

Falconry - using trained birds of prey to hunt animals for sport - is a very ancient practice. It began in China before 1200 BC, and became popular in eastern countries such as India and Arabia very early in their history. In Japan, where falconry was introduced in AD 355, huge areas of the country were set aside as game reserves where falconers went to hunt, and no one else was allowed to go. Until the end of the nineteenth century, falconry was the main reason for wildlife conservation in Japan.

Many rituals grew up around falconry, until it came to be regarded as an art rather than a sport. Falconers had to wear special costumes, and everything had to be done in the right way and at the right time. Trained falcons wear thin straps on their legs, called 'jesses', so that the hunter can hold them on his hand until he is ready to let them fly. In Japan, the colour of these jesses represented the largest bird the falcon had killed. Royal purple jesses could be worn only by a falcon that had killed a Japanese crane, many times its own size. Red, blue, yellow, and brown indicated smaller prey.

Below A mounted falconer in Pakistan carries a goshawk, which he will fly at game birds that have been disturbed by his two assistants.

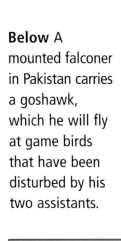

Right This kestrel's eyes are covered with a soft leather hood, tied at the back with a thong and decorated with dyed feathers and plumes. The jesses on its legs are attached to a leash. When it is time to fly, the leash will be removed and the bird unhooded.

GLOSSARY

Bone-marrow The soft material inside a limb bone.

Calories The energy contained in food.

Carnivorous Flesh-eating.

Evolution The gradual change in animals and plants over many generations.

Extinct When a species of animal has died out completely, it is said to be extinct.

Falconer Someone who hunts with trained birds of prey.

Food chain A natural sequence that starts with plants that are eaten by small animals. These are eaten by large animals, which in turn are preyed upon by even larger animals.

Fossil The remains of a long-dead animal or plant that have become part of a rock.

Gosling A young goose.

Kite A bird of prey with long wings and very graceful flight.

Manoeuvrable Able to turn quickly while moving.

Migrate To move long distances from one place to another as the seasons change.

Monogamous Having only one mate.

New World North, South and Central America.

Old World Europe, Africa, and Asia.

Pesticide A poison used to kill destructive insects or unwanted plants.

Plankton Tiny plants and animals that drift in water.

Quill pen A pen made from a bird's wing feather.

Roosting Perching to go to sleep.

Scavenger An animal that feeds on the remains of dead creatures.

Sloth A slow-moving, plant-eating animal that lives in trees in South American forests.

Soar To glide through the air without moving the wings, held up by rising columns of air.

Streamlined Shaped so as to move easily through air or water.

Strychnine A deadly poison.